ISBN:
978-1-7775180-0-4 *Paperback*
978-1-7775180-1-1 *eBook*

Self-Published by Phyllicia LaToya
www.prevailwithlove.com

*Book Design & Cover by Phyllicia LaToya*

*I dedicate this overview to:*


**The Greater Good & Love!**

*Thank you for entrusting me to deliver this strategy and insight to all those who read this overview... May it fulfill all it is meant to!*


**You!**

*Life definitely has its share of challenges, but you are worthy of the journey and deserve to live your authentic best life! May this overview inspire you to broaden your perspective and seek new possibilities!*

# Table Of Contents

# LIFE'S ORIGINAL STRATEGY

## *THE WAY LIFE SHOULD BE!*

Phyllicia LaToya

*www.LifesOriginalStrategy.com**

# Introduction

Life has gotten pretty crazy, hasn't it? Now-a-days, there are so many techniques and strategies for "getting the most out of life". It seems like every celebrity, guru, and influencer, each have a different recipe for success – it is no wonder that most of the world's population is simply surviving instead of living.

Where do you fall on the spectrum of life? Are you happily living life to the fullest, completely satisfied with all that you have accomplished? Do you work hard to make it look like you have got it all together, but really you are dying on the inside? Or are you doing the best you can with what you've got, knowing deep down that you should be doing much better than you are currently?

There must be a method to the madness, right? So, you start looking for help or assistance any way that you can think of and you try to get around like-minded individuals for inspiration and accountability. Sure, it may do the trick in the short term, however more times than not, you find yourself right back where you started – where something is missing... Sound familiar?

Have you ever stopped to consider if life had an "original strategy" what it would look like? I did! – It is absolutely amazing what you discover when you lean into the right source and ask the right questions!

Here is what life shared with me: *Life is systematic, so of course it has an original strategy that can be followed to achieve the optimal life!*

# Life's Original Strategy



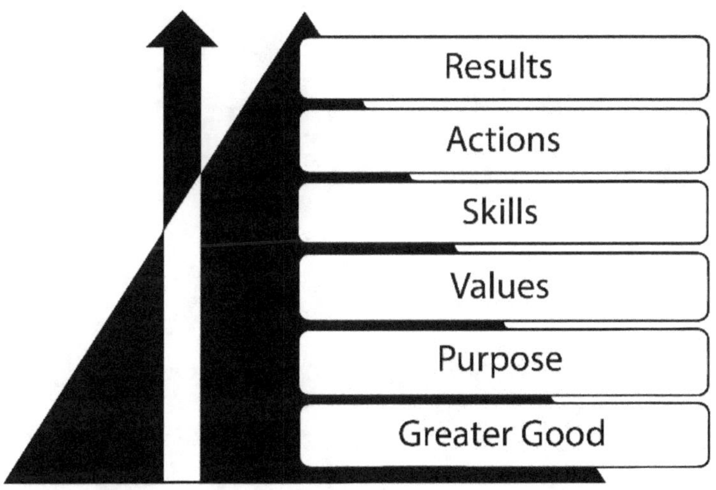



We are to start from the strongest part of the pyramid (the bottom) and work our way up through these fundamentals of life in the appropriate order.

*www.LifesOriginalStrategy.com**

# Greater Good

The term "Greater Good" is self explanatory. It basically means that it is good for humanity as a whole (also known as the "greater") or at the very least, the "bigger picture".

This refers to the fact that everything you do and even think (because your thoughts lead to actions) has a ripple effect that impacts the world/universe in one way or another.

Think about it… Going to the store to buy a shirt, may not seem like a big deal, but that purchase has a ripple effect that often extends to other parts of the world.

You know that expression, "every penny counts"? That is because the $20 shirt you just bought could ripple up to 2000 ($20 x 100 pennies) times. Why? Well, while you are off enjoying your shirt without a care in the world, your $20 gets divided up to cover costs and expenses like labour, marketing, manufacturing, etc. And before your eyes glaze over because of the "business" of it all, just remember that there are people in each of those positions. Your purchase affects the livelihood of each individual involved; some companies hire people from all over the world to do various jobs. – Oh, look at you having a global reach!

Thanks to things like the internet and social media platforms, you don't even need to make a purchase to have an impact on someone else's life. Every post and/or picture stimulates a reaction in all those who see it.

Don't think the little things you do carry such an impact? Think about your childhood… Does anything stand out as something that impacted you (good or bad)? Does that person know the kind of impact that they had on your life? If they did, would they view it with the same impact? Or for them, would their actions be comparable to simply purchasing a shirt?

How do you know if your choices will make a positive impact or a negative one? There is only one way to guarantee that everything will work out positively, and that is to align your entire life with the Greater Good by allowing it to become your *foundation*. When you do, everything becomes a bit easier for two reasons:

1) There is a strange peace and comfort that comes when you witness it all, (both good and bad) work together for the Greater Good.

2) The Greater Good is kind enough to send along Love as a guide to help you navigate through life in the best way possible.

   Love is defined by the Greater Good as the "*natural resource and process of all things good and just*", which means when you are at a crossroad (or really at any point in time), you can choose to lean into Love and listen for its guidance in a way that will benefit everyone fairly in the long term – even if it does not seem like it in the moment or if it comes across as a bit unconventional.

Another benefit to making the Greater Good the foundation of your life is the unshakable stability it provides since nothing can over-throw the Greater Good.

Everything that you build on top of it (in alignment) will indeed last!

It is actually life's ultimate mission to align with the Greater Good. Life's Original Strategy implies that every need would be met, and every resource would be established naturally through the pursuit of the Greater Good.

You will know that this foundation has been achieved when you can honestly and wholeheartedly look through the lens of the Greater Good instead of any one particular person (including yourself). The action steps you take would solely be based on what is best in the long run for the Greater Good instead of an emotion, circumstance, or even logic – this often means taking the road less traveled.

Nonetheless, setting the Greater Good as your solid foundation, and allowing Love

*www.LifesOriginalStrategy.com**

to guide you will ensure that you stay on track by consistently creating checkpoints that pose the question, *"what is the right thing to do?"* So as long as you lean into Love, open yourself up to receive, and remain objective, an answer will always come sooner or later (and often in a way you least expect it to).

# Purpose

The easiest way to define and understand purpose is through arguably the most powerful question in the world… *"Why?"*

Why is the universal question that is designed to get to the heart and intention – you know the purpose – of anything really. It often stimulates thought provoking opportunities to deepen understanding, gain perspective (or direction), and discover the root cause.

Most leaders in the Self-Help space will stress the importance of having a "why" – a vision big enough to motivate you into action and get you up in the morning. The problem is that this only tends to work for a period of time, and the fire from that vision usually burns out eventually (which may leave you second guessing yourself or giving up on it all together). The reason for this is because nine times out of ten, you will create your goals and/or vision out of thin air; based on what makes sense to you in a particular season of your life.

What happens when your life shifts or you encounter an obscene amount of opposition? Automatically, that same vision shifts as well and sometimes sends you into a completely different direction. When that happens, you will most likely remember what you have been taught and count it all as learning or growing pains.

The fact-of-the-matter is that you would be going through the same thing over and over again by creating a new "why" out of thin air, your life shifts, then your vision changes, and you find yourself right back where you started – just with more "life lessons".

Here's the thing: ABSOLUTELY EVERYTHING AND EVERYONE HAS A SPECIFIC PURPOSE – a *reason* it was created. Therefore, it is paramount to know the reason for your own existence <u>before</u> you attempt to create a vision for your future.

Can you imagine a flower rising every morning to declare that it is going to become a basketball All-Star?... A flower, as an All-Star?...

Well, we do live in a world where anything is possible and although the flower may not become a household name, it could find its way to the bottom of an All-Star's shoe and potentially see the inside of the arena. But let's be real, do you see how absurd that flower's vision really is?

Not because the dream of becoming a basketball All-Star isn't a worthy one to have, but because it is so far from the flower's intended purpose that even after putting in the effort to shift its mindset and learn new skills, the best it could do was to end up at the bottom of a shoe…

Why settle? No matter how much success you think you can have within a purpose you create out of thin air (or logic), it will never amount to the way you will thrive (with least resistance) when you don't *create* your "why" at all, and instead seek to <u>understand</u> it.

Try asking yourself some of these very important questions (fill in the blanks and answer):

- Why am I on this planet?
- Why am I talented in ____?
- Why am I passionate about ____?

- Why does ___ bother me?
- Why does ___ bring me joy?
- Why does ___ intrigue me?
- Why do I desire ___?

For every answer you come up with, simply ask: "why is that important?" because your initial response brought your answers to the surface, however, if you want to get to the core of your purpose you will have to dig deeper until you get there. – By the way, "I don't know" (or any variation of that) is considered unacceptable.

Here's an example of what that conversation with self could look like:

"Why am I passionate about writing?" *"Well, I was a quiet kid, so writing became a quiet form of expression for me, like an outlet."*

*www.LifesOriginalStrategy.com**

"Why is that important?" *"I guess I really got good at organizing my crazy, innovative thoughts on paper."*

"Okay, and why is that important?" *"Um, it has helped me properly process, simplify, and understand all sorts of crazy things in my life."*

"Hm, why is that important?" *"Well, it has given me the necessary skills to dissect some of life's toughest questions and the ability to effectively communicate my findings in a way where those who need it most understand it."* – Let's stop here…

The moment you dig deep enough and come up with a genuine, heartfelt response that impacts other people, you have reached the core. Now you have to do a check to see if it truly is meant to be a part of your purpose. You can check with these two questions:

1) Do my findings align with the Greater Good? (Lean into your guide, Love, for a response.)

2) Is this meant to be a part of my life's purpose?

After the Greater Good, Life's Original Strategy needs to ensure that you understand the specific role you play within the grand scheme of things.

You are a logical being (life gets that), which is why it will always take you through a journey of self-discovery. So do not avoid it, or try to run from it, just embrace the journey!

Sure, there will be things that you won't want to deal with, and there will be other things that you thought you dealt with that will rear its ugly head all over again, but using the Greater Good as your foundation and Love as your guide to uncover your true purpose means that once you have stepped into who you are meant to be, you will most likely obtain new wisdom and insights that will cause you to deal with the things of your past differently. It should also allow you to confidently look into the mirror, and love what you see staring back at you! Living a life from that place is definitely one worth fighting for…

# Values

Essentially, values represent your rules for engagement – how you choose to show up in this world. It is all about perception and what you deem worthy of your time and/or investment. However, true value is what is at the heart of those actions.

Ultimately, your values act as the center of gravity for your life because the point at which all of your true values align is where you will find balance. What you say, do, and experience is the direct result of how aligned you are with your true values in association with the Greater Good and your purpose.

Consider your values to be the destination point in your life's Global Positioning System (GPS). As you hop in your car and head towards your destination (your values), you will hear your inner guide (Love) navigating the directions for the best possible route. Sometimes, unexpected things occur, like closures or missed opportunity, and you are forced to take a different route than expected. Your GPS (Greater Good and Love) will not abandon you, instead they will help you "re-route" and find the best possible way from where you are.

Basically, your values are your life's focal point (whether you realize it or not), and what you focus on is the direction your life will head in. So, the real question is, *"what do you focus on?"*

Is it the past? If so, that would be like choosing to drive your car in reverse all the way to your destination, only to find out that you have really been driving in circles. You probably got so tired of hearing your guide say, "re-routing" that you silenced the voice all together and are attempting to figure it out on your own while staring out your rear-view mirror. How has that honestly been working for you?

Maybe you choose to value money or material possessions? Sure, they are a necessity to life's functionality, however if you set them as your final destination, the best you would do after fighting through all of the challenges that come along with your journey, would be to end up at a bank or a mall in a fancy car…

Then what would you do after closing time? – That is metaphorically asking, *"do you want to be known for choosing money and stuff when you pass on, even though you cannot take any of it with you?"*

Of course, you could argue, "I'm providing", which would be true and appreciated. However, if it becomes your sole focal point, would that mean you would rather provide than live?

The truth is, neither one of these examples would be considered a *true value* because those are surface level perceptions and there are core level reasons that have yet to be explored. This is where that powerful universal question comes in again, *"why?"* ...

Why do you focus on the past?... Maybe it is shame, hurt, regret, unforgiveness, etc. ...

Why do you focus on money and/or material things?... Maybe it is fear, guilt, greed, etc. ... Or maybe you feel insecure...

The reality is that there is almost always at least one core reason behind the day-to-day things that you focus on. It is that core reason that becomes your true value and gets entered into your life's GPS.

There is good news: you ALWAYS have a choice! That is the beautiful thing about free will! You get to choose what values you input into your GPS, which means that you can change them at any point in time. Although, it is important to be very mindful of your circumstances and environment because if you take a detour and decide to stay there too long, you may end up changing your final destination as well without even realizing it. So, the number one thing to remember about values is that *'when you compromise your values, you compromise your destiny'.*

This is the reason why Life's Original Strategy requires you to align with the Greater Good and your purpose <u>before</u> considering your values. It is to ensure that when you do choose your values, they are ones that you can truly be proud of, and therefore you are less likely to waiver from them when times get tough.

You see, the Greater Good already has a set list of true values that it operates from. However, that full list might never become available as this is not an 'à la carte', where you get to pick and choose what looks good to you. Instead, it is about discovering the true values that will bring *your purpose* to life, so that you can embody all that you need to on behalf of the Greater Good.

For some, one true value is all they need to fulfill their purpose, and that is just the right amount for them! There is also a rare few who will embody all of the Greater Good's values, however, humility is one of those values, so the likelihood of you being able to identify one of those people would be really slim. The mass majority of people will have several true values that intersect at a very specific point.

Everyone's journey looks different because each person is uniquely made. Nonetheless, there is a gravitational pull that naturally unites people with the same true values. So, as you venture out along the streets of life, be sure to stay in your lane, and keep an eye out for those who strive to embody the same true values as you…

# Skills

Your skills are the set of traits (born with) and abilities (learned) that you choose to use in order to fulfill your purpose. Skills can be developed and/or mastered over time, therefore, the most important factors when deciding which skills to use are passion and desire.

Using a skill simply because you are good at it will tire over time, whereas doing something you are passionate about will motivate you to never give up on it so that it will stand the test of time. Passion and desire also breed creativity and innovation, which means your skills will continue to grow and mature just as you do.

Selecting your skills should not be something you take lightly. The reality is that life's journey is not an easy one and so your skills will be tried and tested. There will be challenging days, so if you are not fully committed to your skills, your journey becomes even more difficult unnecessarily.

A rule of thumb to ensure that you are on the right path would be to consider whether you would be blissfully happy using that skill everyday for the rest of your life and not get paid to do so. If "no" would be your answer, then you may want to think about using a different skill.

Consider viewing your skills as ingredients to your 'recipe for life'. There will always be one or two main ingredients (those are the ones you will need to have a deep desire for), and then a bunch of other ingredients to fulfill other various purposes. Individually, each of your skills may be good, however it is only when you combine all of your chosen skills together in your unique way that you will see the 'magic' start to happen!

So, what skills do you currently have? What are you passionate about? What were some things you loved to do as a kid? If you had all of the money you could ever want in the world, and you had the time to master one skill, which skill would it be?

Still not sure what your chosen skills should be? That is okay! As you become more aligned with the Greater Good, your purpose, and your values, the skills best suited for you will become more evident. At times, you may notice that the things you loved to do as a kid naturally, or the things you had the biggest challenges around will end up being the very skill you will need to fulfill your purpose.

The main reason for this struggle is relatability. Your triumphant journey of how you overcame your challenges in order to use your skills, is the very thing that will attract people to you and inspire others to overcome their challenges as well. In other words, it is not just about how good you are at your skill, it is also about your journey, and what you are willing to do with that skill.

It can be scary to use your skills, gifts, and talents publicly. Sometimes the fear can be quite intimidating, and you may find that there are other times where you just do not feel like you are enough or capable.

Those feelings are normal, and everyone faces moments like that at one point or another. The key is to rise above those feelings and embrace the vulnerability by recognizing that you really are able and capable of anything you set your mind to. You are also worthy of and can handle all the good things that come your way for using your skills accordingly in what ever capacity you have been assigned to by the Greater Good.

Life's Original Strategy uses this stage to help you prepare for the work that is ahead of you, and helps you develop a game plan for the best way for you to use your skills in alignment to the Greater Good through your purpose and values.

Since each stage builds upon the one before, it should be very clear by now that *alignment is very important* and should be taken very seriously if you would like this strategy to work for you.

No matter what happens along the way, ALWAYS EXPECT THE UNEXPECTED, and remember that you are the one who gets to design and customize the framework for that journey.

So, be sure to trust in the very skills and abilities that make you wonderfully, and uniquely you!...

# Actions

Anything you do and/or execute would be considered an action. Having the knowledge of your skills, values, and purpose is great, but pointless unless you actually do something with that information. And honestly, it is not good enough to take action just for the sake of doing something – that is how you guarantee wasted time and frustration.

Every step you take should be *intentional* because the energy and effort you put into anything matters. It determines how you show up and execute your plans.

The expectation of your outcome also matters which is why it is important for you to always expect good things to happen. Even if it turns out you failed, the feeling of defeat should only be temporary, so that you can objectively learn the life lesson from the failure and begin to make those necessary change(s) to improve the chances of a better outcome on your next set of action steps.

It is vital for your actions to align with your values as this alignment creates authenticity. Taking a stand for what you believe in is not usually an easy thing to do. Actually, it is often the road less travelled, which means you may face bigger obstacles for standing up for yourself and your values than you would have if you compromised. Should you choose that path, keep in mind that when you compromise your values, you compromise your destiny, and it is through your actions by doing things that do not align with your values that causes you to compromise in the first place.

Being authentic requires you to prove yourself, so the journey may take a bit longer, however you will almost always be rewarded for your efforts. When you learn to become the authentic best version of yourself in alignment with the Greater Good, new doors and opportunities tend to fly open naturally. Tough decisions in the beginning usually leads to benefits that will stand the test of time.

When it comes to action, farming is a great example to provide an illustration because of its concept of seedtime and harvest:

A farmer, when planting seeds into the soil, expects those seeds to grow healthy so that they can harvest their crops in due season and reap the rewards of their efforts… If a farmer plants wheat, does he then expect corn to grow? No! He expects wheat and will get wheat come harvest time. The point is, what he puts into the soil is typically what he will get out of it.

Life is your soil; your actions are your seeds. If you take action steps that compromise your values, how can you expect to live your best life when you have planted seeds that were designed to create an unstable foundation?

If you want a foundation for your life that is a bit more stable, don't you think you should take the necessary steps to ensure your actions reflect that?

The same can be said for inaction or choosing to sacrifice your purpose for the sake of others. It would be like a farmer holding onto a seed so tightly that she never lets it fall to the ground – yet hoping and wishing for her harvest to come. How would that even be possible when the seed never left her hand?

Are you afraid of taking action that aligns with your purpose/values? Do you keep putting others before yourself? Are you wishing for your dreams to come true, but have not been doing anything to get you there?

The truth is, action can be scary and with so many different variables to take into account, there are times when action can feel a bit overwhelming. Luckily, there are two very important things you can keep in mind that should help you better navigate:

1) Pursue. Learn. Adjust... One step at a time – All you really need to concern yourself with in each moment is the *next right move*. Once you have a target put blinders on to block out everything

and everyone else so you can pursue it with confidence. If it was a success, great! You did it!... If it was a failure, that is great too! Learn from it and make the necessary change to your plans. That way you can adjust your next step in a way where you can pursue it differently, then just continue this cycle *(Pursue. Learn. Adjust.)* until you see your desired outcome.

Think about it… How would you climb a huge mountain? One step at a time. So, if you focus on how big the mountain is and what it is really going to take for you to climb it, you will most likely get discouraged, and want to delay or completely dismiss your objective of climbing the mountain entirely.

However, if you simply focus on what your next right step should be, while working up the courage and strength to take that step regardless of any challenges you may be up against, then you would find yourself at the top of that mountain sooner rather than later. That is because all of those little steps will begin to add up quickly, momentum will begin to transpire, and the mountain that seemed like it was utterly impossible to conquer, all of a sudden became possible!

2) Persevere – No matter what happens, you have to find a way to keep pushing through until you pass the finish line.

The only guarantees in life are the ones that you set for yourself. So, if you guarantee yourself success on your dreams and aspirations, you <u>cannot</u> stop until you get where you need to be. If you give up (and unfortunately, there are various reasons as to why most people give up *just before* they reach their goal), you guarantee your failure. Sometimes a fresh perspective and a few minor adjustments are all that is needed to turn a failure into a success, but you have to be opened to those possibilities in order to receive the learning from the lessons of your journey. The faster you learn those lessons and <u>apply them to your life</u>, the faster you get to move on to new levels.

For Life's Original Strategy, action is considered movement and movement is essential to progression. There are three components to movement: a 'seeing' (your perception – what you envision), a 'knowing' (your beliefs – what you plan), and a 'doing' (your actions – what you execute). Some movement can seem automatic or instant because there is a quick transition between these three components, whereas other movements require careful analysis for a proper strategy to ensure the actions taken would be most beneficial.

So, some food for thought to gain insight on how you currently move would be to ask yourself, "does what I see affect what I know, which then affects what I do?" Or "am I the type of person who does what I know, regardless of what I see?"

These are two very different approaches to life: one is morally sound, where the other is morally compromised…

Which one are you? And does it align with the Greater Good? – The Greater Good will always ask you to stand for what is right and fight for what is morally sound.

Ultimately, life is what you make it, so take the necessary action steps to ensure that you get to live a life worth living!

# Results

Results are the outcome of your efforts, the fruit of your labour, and the environment of your choices. Each one of those represents a valuable part in the overall result of life and cover the three most important bases: Body/Physical (the fruit of your labour), Mind/Mental (the environment of your choices), and Soul/Spiritual (the outcome of your efforts).

Each of these components are equal in valued importance, however there is an ideal order:

1) Soul/Spiritual – This is your direct connection with the Greater Good and its guide, Love. Establishing this relationship first will help you in so many different (and powerful) ways. Since Love is the

*'natural resource and process of all things good and just'*, the fundamental need of hope becomes evident because striving to align with Love means that in one way or another all the good and bad (everything) will work out for the best in the end.

It is that hope (through Love) and the understanding that you are a part of the collective (Greater Good) and that will help to keep you on track, motivate you to push through every obstacle, and help you fight for what you believe in.

2) Mind/Mental – This is where you create that connection with yourself. Embarking on a true self-love journey will help you better understand your own identity and

purpose in accordance with the Greater Good. It will help to shift your mindset. Once awareness emerges and you step into your best authentic self, then your mental health typically improves drastically, and you are able to make wiser decisions. This is also where tools like confidence, resilience, and influence, etc. are developed so they can be ready for use when you need them the most.

Ultimately, it is at this stage that you learn to find and to keep your focus.

3) Body/Physical – This is the proof that makes the connection with the world. Everything that has been done mentally and spiritually

will manifest physically in one way or another. Being that this is the third phase, there is often a delay since things tend to shift within the soul and then the mind long before it becomes evident in the body.

That being said, when you take care of your external properties and/or environment, you will in turn empower yourself to even greater heights because what happens on the outside often affects what happens on the inside. However, there is a fine line that is supposed to balance everything out.

Striving to live in and create harmony between the mind, body and soul should be a key objective on your life's journey because it is ideal for optimal support and functionality.

Consider this… Would it do you any good to sit in a room and do nothing but read in an attempt to expand your mind all day, every day for a week straight? How would you feel afterwards?

Most likely tired from not sleeping, weak from not eating or drinking, and numb from not making connections or moving purposefully (if you even made it through the week) …

Focusing solely on one area while neglecting the other two does more of a disservice than anything else. All three categories need to be functioning and cared for simultaneously in order for the best results to appear. Once there is synchronicity, you should be able to fulfill your purpose with least resistance for

*www.LifesOriginalStrategy.com**

optimal results. – Yes, opposition will still occur as no one is immune to challenges, however those challenges will no longer defeat you and instead, be purposed to move you into your next level in life.

So, are you currently receiving the results you desire out of life? Have you pursued results in the correct order by establishing your soul, mind, then body? Do you currently experience balance between your mind, body, and soul? What is it that you need to shift now in order to establish your desired results in the future?

It is easy to look at your environment and then pin-point various things you would like to change. More times than not, you may be tempted to do something that would equate to a quick fix, while hoping that change lasts.

Unfortunately, that is the worst thing you could do because in the same way that you should not judge a book by its cover, you should not judge a life by its environment. Attempting to fix the physical directly will only lead to temporary solutions.

Have you ever thought, "maybe if I learn this skill or shift my mindset then things will finally change"? Then you put in all of the work and trust the process only for things to fail and/or blow up in your face…

The reason for that is because there are millions of different things you could learn to improve your current mindset and/or skills, so the likelihood of you blindly selecting the best option for yourself is very slim (think odds of winning the lottery) …

It is great that you understand the power of your mind, however attempting to fix the mental in order to fix the physical is only part of the equation and therefore it will also establish a temporary solution. – Why gamble with your life?

For best results and lasting solutions, always begin with a spiritual realignment with the Greater Good and re-establish a strong relationship with its guide, Love. Not only does Love have phenomenal navigational skills, it is also quite the encourager, troubleshooter, and warrior!

Only once you have created a solid spiritual foundation, should you move onto forming a solid mental state. What matters most here is that you believe you are mentally sound in your own unique way. – As long as you continue to abide by the necessary laws and are not hurting anyone in any way (including yourself), then it is okay for people to think that you are 'off your rockers' for simply being you.

There must be a season that is all about aligning mentally with what is best for you, not what is best for others. And surprisingly enough in the long run, you will find that what is best for you usually ends up being the best for others as well.

A sound mind that is spiritually aligned is the best foundation strong enough to sustain all of your physical needs. The majority of your action steps will most likely be intentional and therefore should manifest the desires of your heart accordingly.

Results is the final stage in Life's Original Strategy. Life almost called this section "rewards" because no matter how you interacted with each phase, and regardless of how aligned they are with one another in your life, you are still "rewarded" for your efforts (or lack thereof) appropriately.

So, if you made the effort to follow Life's Original Strategy, then you would have laid the proper foundation for your wildest dreams to come true. However, if you chose another path, then your life would reflect that and no matter how successful you become with this path, feelings of dissatisfaction or a void where it often feels like something is missing, almost always leads to self-destruction.

Life has finally provided you with its *original strategy,* so the question now becomes, *"what are you going to do with this information?"*

You are valuable, and you are destined to become the absolute best version of yourself in whatever capacity that may be! The world is waiting for the best version of you to emerge!

*Please don't keep us waiting…*

*www.LifesOriginalStrategy.com**

# *Are you ready to use Life's Original Strategy to reorganize your life?*

This book was an overview designed to help you start with the end in mind. It provided brief descriptions, key objectives, and simple strategies to effectively outline Life's Original Strategy.

Truth be told, we have barely scratched the surface, and since life is meant to be interactive, merely reading about it would not give you the life you desire.

That is why I have created various tools and resources for each strategy to assist you in better understanding Life's Original Strategy and how to implement it into your life, regardless of your starting point! (You're welcome!) ...

*www.LifesOriginalStrategy.com**

# Next Steps

### *CUSTOMIZE YOUR EXPERIENCE!*

A questionnaire designed to help you create awareness around where you are currently in life, so you can identify your starting point and customize your experience based on your needs and goals, is available to you!

1) To access the questionnaire, visit: **www.LifesOriginalStrategy.com***

2) Once online, scroll down. Click on: **"Start The Questionnaire Here!"**

3) Then answer the questions as honestly, and thoroughly as possible.

   *(This process should compel you to ask yourself some of the tough*

*questions, leaving room to reveal how connected you currently are with Life's Original Strategy.)*

4) When complete, take a minute to make note of how you feel in the moment, and consider why that is.

5) Over the next few days, keep an eye on your inbox for various tools, resources, and ways to connect.

*(Please note, that processing times vary, so if you have not received something after a week, feel free to send an email to life@lifesoriginalstrategy.com*, but please check your junk mail first).*

# Free Resources

## Available To All

A FREE Newsletter where you will receive one new strategy to implement along with useful food for thought to help you deepen your understanding of the key stages of Life's Original Strategy.

To subscribe, please visit this site: **www.LifesOriginalStrategy.com***

*(Once subscribed, you will also receive access to a variety of tools and resources as they become available for added support on your journey!)*

## Private Community

The private community is a FREE resource that is available to those who have a desire to explore Life's Original Strategy in depth and discover new and amazing things about life!

This community is <u>not</u> for everyone, which is why the successful completion of *Life's Original Strategy Questionnaire* is a mandatory requirement in order to be considered.

To start the process, please visit:
**www.LifesOriginalStrategy.com***

* If for whatever reason the link(s) does not work, please email life@lifesoriginalstrategy.com, do a web search on Phyllicia LaToya to find contact information or visit www.prevailwithlove.com and let me know about the error in one way or another, so it can be corrected as soon as possible. This is far too important for technical errors to hinder the process. Thank you in advance for helping to maintain this resource for all who need it. You are appreciated and valued!

www.ingramcontent.com/pod-product-compliance
Lightning Source LLC
Chambersburg PA
CBHW051008050726
47592CB00007B/2757